Open Your Mind, Open Your Heart

Open Your Mind, Open Your Heart

A collection of words of wisdom, heartfelt thoughts, and original poetry

by
W. Marie Giles

Open Your Mind, Open Your Heart

Copyright 2003 by W. Marie Giles

All rights reserved. No part of this book may be used or reproduced in any manner whatsoever without the written permission of the Publisher.

Unless otherwise noted, scripture taken from the HOLY BIBLE, NEW INTERNATIONAL VERSION®. Copyright 1973, 1978, 1984 by International Bible Society. Used by permission of Zondervan Publishing House. All rights reserved.

The "NIV" and "New International Version" trademarks are registered in the United States Patent and Trademark Office by International Bible Society. Use of either trademark requires the permission of International Bible Society.

Library of Congress Control Number: 2003094793

ISBN: 0-9728944-0-3

Cover design: W. Marie Giles
Book layout design: W. Marie Giles
Cover photo: Vickie Bushee

Printed in the United States of America

When you open your mind and open your heart, the possibilities for a more fulfilling life are endless.

Acknowledgement

I wish to graciously thank all my friends and family for encouraging me to reach for my dreams.

I am especially grateful for my co-workers who previewed many of my works, as I tested the waters of their opinions.

I am most grateful to God for not only giving me the gifts and the inspiration to create from words but also for the desire to share these gifts with others who may appreciate them and benefit, perhaps in some small measure, from what I have been granted.

To those whose lives I have touched, I appreciate your kindness and reception.

To those whose lives I have yet to touch, I look forward to the experience.

Foreword

Somewhere in my life, I was told to accommodate others before myself. It was suggested this is the way to *make it* and get others to like and accept you.

At a later point, after embarking on the path of self-discovery, I learned that I, in fact, had a gift for listening to others and making them feel important. I came to accept this as who I am. I continued to explore my inner self and always came up with the same characteristics. In my collection of self-help, motivational, and inspirational materials, I am always pulled to the same center. This is evidence to me that I know who I am, why I do the things I do, and what my true purpose is in life.

I have learned that I cannot expect to be nurtured in the way that I have nurtured others. However, most importantly, I have learned that the nurturing I *need* comes from God and from my very act of nurturing others – not to be accepted or liked, but rather to be me.

Because of this validation, I know my gifts have been given to be shared and to improve the lives of others and, therefore, obtain the nurturing I require. This premise encourages me to be grateful for my gifts and to continually look for ways to share them. It helps me focus on unselfish acts – not expecting payment in money or other material items. The sheer satisfaction I gain from brightening someone's day, improving someone's outlook, or simply changing someone's direction is more than I ever hope to earn pursuing my chosen profession.

My objective in sharing these thoughts is not to encourage you to "be like me". What I would challenge you to do is embark upon your own *self-discovery*. It is incumbent upon each of us to determine who we really are and what gifts we have to share. I am convinced that each person is placed upon this earth for a purpose. Whether it is to transform, be transformed, or both, you must explore for yourself. Once learned, each day becomes truly meaningful in a way that is inexplicable to those yet untouched.

Dedication

This book is dedicated to my husband, Henry, and our sons, Hendric Le-Mar and Westin Marele. You have made my life worth living and, but for you, I would not be who I am nor would I have lived my life the way I have. I love you dearly and hope I have been able to add a dimension to your lives, the likes of which you may never erase from your minds and hearts.

For my Mother, who left this earthly existence on 25 July 2001: I am always grateful for your teachings of patience, fairness, confidence, trustworthiness, and a positive outlook on life.

About the Author

W. Marie Giles is a wife and working mother of two boys. She has been on a journey of self-discovery and self-improvement nearly all her life. She has come to realize the journey does not end, for "it is in the journey that you continue to improve your outlook and reach a higher level of fulfillment."

Marie's chosen profession is in the field of Information Technology where she currently works as a senior manager in government service.

She resides in Pensacola, Florida, with her husband and two sons.

Contents

Part I — Words of Wisdom and Heartfelt Thoughts

Chapter 1— Be Positive! 16

> Be aware of, concerned about, and sensitive to the impact of your negative behavior, actions, words, and attitude on others. 20
>
> Regularly show your loved-ones how much you care. 24
>
> Don't discourage your loved-ones from showing you how much they care by being unapproachable or emotionally unavailable. 26
>
> Choose kind words, especially with children, rather than hurtful ones. 28
>
> Recognize and acknowledge the things others do to please or show concern for you or show you they care. 30
>
> View your relationships as partnerships. Give equal value to your spouse, siblings, employers, subordinates, friends, children, and parents as you give yourself. 32
>
> Seek out the good in others rather than dwelling on their negative traits. 34

Do what you say you are going to do rather than just saying it. Acts and deeds sway and impress far more than words and speeches. 38

Be aware of how you are painting the portrait of your life. It will live long after you are gone. It's how you will be remembered. 40

Don't hold it against those who know not or use not politeness. His misery is evident in the lack there of. Ignore it and don't return the act. 44

When insults bounce off you, they boomerang. When you ignore or overlook insults, the act returns to the sender. 46

Change yourself to change your life. 48

Accepting weakness shows strength. 50

Unresolved anger, deep within you, is not hidden. It is revealed in your thoughts, words, and actions. It controls your very existence. 52

You ALWAYS have a choice and the choice is yours. 54

Simple acts of kindness are like boomerangs— they come back to you. 56

Trust is KEY. 58

A promise kept enhances trust. 62

Honesty matters. 64

Reach for your dreams, even if you have to stand on your tiptoes. 66

Part II—Original Poetry

Chapter 2 — Open Your Mind 70

    The Lesson 71

    Stop the Anger! 72

    Fate 73

    For Everything A Reason 74

    A Need To Know 76

    Optimism/Pessimism 77

    Boundaries 78

    Undisputed 80

    Angels 81

    Lessons Learned? 83

Chapter 3 — Open Your Heart 84

    Kindness 85

With Each New Day 87

If 89

Is That Really Me? 91

Without Words? 92

The Circle Of Love 94

What You Mean To Me 95

Everyone Has A Story To Tell 96

Within My Heart 97

We're All They Have Left 98

Chapter 4 — Open Your Mind and Your Heart 100

My Time Is Done 101

My Reward 102

Epilog—Life Through Books 104

After Word 106

PART I

Words of Wisdom and Heartfelt Thoughts

Chapter 1

Be Positive!

"Don't be narrow-minded."
"Keep an open mind."
"Don't be a skeptic."
"Accentuate the positive."

Do these expressions sound familiar? You may not hear them often but they are shared by many positive people. Beginning to live with a positive outlook on life takes effort. All around, everyday events beckon us to take part in negative interactions -- at home, work, school, with spouses, parents, children, and coworkers. The influences are so great that negative reactions become the natural response – without any forethought.

Sometimes, even if the stimulus does not indicate a negative reaction, it's given anyway. Soon, you may reach a point where you thrive on the negative.

Some encounters begin positively enough. However, before long, perhaps to maintain control or impress others, it turns sour. You end up being sarcastic, talking about others who are not present (behind their backs), or you start rumors you know are untrue. The puzzling thing about all this is, it doesn't really make you or anyone else happy. You're miserable and want others to keep you company.

Sounds bleak? Perhaps, but not hopeless. All it takes is a single person to begin a new cycle of positive thoughts and acts. You could very well be that person. Start by refusing to get pulled into constant negatives.

Don't expect others to blindly follow suit or cease their negative behavior. And don't despair if their response is not what you want it to be. Just remember that the longest journey begins with a single step just as the hardest job begins with a single task, and the greatest oak began as a small acorn. The greatest change begins within yourself.

On the following pages are thoughts to help you develop a more positive outlook on life. They have been compiled from personal experience, observations of others, and the desire for a more enjoyable and fulfilling life.

Think Positive!

Live Positive!

Be Positive!

__Open-Mindedness__

Ready acceptance of new suggestions, ideas, influences, or opinions.

Capable of entertaining new ideas without skepticism or prejudice; free-thinking; showing respect for the rights, opinions, or practices of others, even if they are different from your own.

Be aware of, concerned about, and sensitive to the impact of your negative behavior, actions, words, and attitude on others.

When you make an effort to become more aware of how your negative actions, words, and attitude impact others, you may uncover a source of your own frustration and unhappiness. Until you do, you may blame others for reacting adversely to these behaviors.

Once aware, you may have enough concern to adjust any offending behaviors in order to reverse the accompanying reaction from others. You will experience an inward sensitivity toward others that will bring closeness to your personal relationships. Your professional relationships will also benefit.

Don't ignore obvious reactions to your offending behaviors. Sometimes, people may tend to avoid you in order to prevent any unpleasant interactions with you. Or, they may appear to exhibit matching defensive behavior in reaction to yours.

In some instances, offended parties may harbor revenge against you, seizing any opportunity to sabotage your honest efforts in other areas. Try noticing the body language, voice tone, facial expressions, or even the failure of others to respond to you. These may reveal important cues on how your behavior is impacting others.

Self-Observe!

Self-Observation

To see or sense oneself, especially through directed careful analytic attention.

To take notice of one's own behavior, attitude, thoughts, words, and actions.

Regularly show your loved-ones how much you care.

Family and close friends care about you and want to feel you care for them. Mention it occasionally. Don't mince words or neglect taking actions because you think it's not appropriate or shows weakness. People, in general, want to feel they are important and are appreciated. Let them know it. Don't just say it – show it!

Don't discourage your loved-ones from showing you how much they care by being unapproachable or emotionally unavailable.

Be emotionally available – not just physically. You may seem unapproachable to others when you are either unresponsive or react without consideration. Also, if you regularly appear annoyed when those you love attempt to offer endearments or want to spend time with you, they become discouraged and resolve to withdraw from you emotionally and, perhaps, even physically.

When, on the other hand, you realize that your physical presence is not all that's needed, your relationships will begin to improve. Communication with others will not seem so strained or superficial. You will begin to see how much influence you have in creating a more positive environment at home as well as at work.

Choose kind words, especially with children, rather than hurtful ones.

Kind words garner far more than hurtful ones. Children, especially, don't understand when they are constantly put down without the benefit of a meaningful lesson. They begin to see themselves through your eyes even though your intentions may not be such.

Many children are so sensitive that even occasional slurs are taken to heart.

On the other hand, when you practice kindness, you show there is value in the individual that merits such treatment. The return on this investment could be immeasurable.

Recognize and acknowledge the things others do to please or show concern for you or show you they care.

Don't be casual or negative in expressing your appreciation for considerate deeds received by you. Acknowledge the giver, showing them that you recognize the thought or action on your behalf.

When someone realizes that you appreciate them or what they do for you, they will continue to shower you with this attention. Your life will change in a positive way just by acknowledging someone else.

View your relationships as partnerships. Give equal value to your spouse, siblings, employers, subordinates, friends, children, and parents as you give to yourself.

Realize that all persons deserve the same respect and consideration from you that you expect from them. Value their opinions even if you don't agree with them. Try to find a common purpose on which to build solid relationships in your personal as well as professional life. Value the differences in others that can serve to complement your own. Accept that you don't know all you need to know and you can't do everything yourself.

"No man is an island", is a common expression that applies here. Whenever you look at others as having valuable contributions to situations or issues you face, you create a win-win solution. Decisions, as well as their benefits (or consequences), become jointly owned by you and all contributors. You will rise above the "mine" or "me" and "theirs" or "them" mentality, to a point where you think "we", "us", and "ours".

Seek out the good in others rather than dwelling on their negative traits.

When you focus on other than the positive, you tend to react to those traits. Everyone has something positive to offer and it takes someone who cares enough to recognize it in even the most negative of subjects. It's worth it to see a transformation in someone whom others felt incapable of showing such positive behavior.

Most people tend to migrate toward what they are constantly told they are – good or bad. You can influence how someone perceives himself by giving him negative or positive reinforcements. If someone receives constant negatives, they will tend to see themselves that way.

On the other hand, if you focus on the positive traits, however small, you may begin to see changes in how people perceive themselves. This does not happen overnight and requires constant focusing on your part. If you stop at the first sign of regression, you miss an opportunity to make a difference in the life of someone else.

Not all things happen exactly how or when we want them to. Additionally, sustained success requires continuous application of efforts. You don't relax once you have reached the top position. You have to continue to work to remain there. Likewise, you can't give up at the first sign of failure by those you want to help turn their lives around.

When someone sees your continued efforts, it shows them that you value positive change in them and have confidence enough to take a chance on sticking with them.

Focus on the Positive!

Do what you say you are going to do rather than just saying it. Acts and deeds sway and impress far more than words and speeches.

People are far more confident in those who do what they say they will do than in those who give only lip service. When others have confidence in you it raises your credibility and therefore, your own self-esteem. Your reputation will precede you and reduce your need to constantly prove yourself. You'll earn the respect you feel you deserve.

If you can't or won't follow through with something, don't say you will. If, for some reason, you make every visible, honest attempt and fail, you will be perceived as at least having tried. That counts for something.

Be aware of how you are painting the portrait of your life. It will live long after you are gone. It's how you will be remembered.

How you live is how you will be remembered. Give serious thought to what will be said about you at your funeral, in the workplace, and in your social groups. What accomplishments did you make that benefited others? What significant contributions did you make to society? How did you treat your fellowman? Your family? Your friends? Did you live your life with a purpose?

Once you leave this earthly existence, how would you like to be remembered? Try writing down some of the things you would like your spouse and children to convey to the person who delivers your eulogy. Include things you want to be remembered for by your coworkers and friends.

As you attend and listen to the words of remembrance at the funerals of others, think about your own funeral. Is there something in the minister's words that gives you comfort? What do you think the bereaved are thinking? Is there something that gives them comfort? What can be said at your own funeral to give your family and friends the comfort they seek to keep you in their hearts and minds? What legacy can you leave that will be carried on or help them accept your passing on?

These are serious things to think about. You can have a direct and positive influence on how you will be put to rest long before that fateful day arrives.

Live your life with a purpose!

Who are you and why are you here on earth right now?
What are you doing and why are you doing it at this time?

What is your true purpose in life?

Don't hold it against those who know not or use not politeness. His misery is evident in the lack thereof. Ignore it and don't return the act.

Don't return acts of impoliteness with the same. It benefits no one. When someone is impolite to you, so often you react to it without stopping first to think about it. Consider this act as a stimulus. Now view the time between this stimulus and your response as being enough for you to think about what you say before you actually say it. Consider that there is enough time in between to think about a response that will not perpetuate impoliteness any further than the individual who delivers it. Sometimes, no response may be the best response. It may be just what it takes to disarm the offender.

The key to accomplishing this is to be consciously aware, all the time, of how you respond to stimuli. Take time to think about it. Consider how your response will be received. What do you want to accomplish? Let the answer to that question guide you in your response.

When insults bounce off you, they boomerang. When you ignore or overlook insults, the act returns to the sender.

If you refuse to react to an insult it has no where to go but back to the offender. By your not reacting, the offender is disarmed.

Much time and effort are wasted on futile attempts to match insults with offenders.

Sometimes insults are a cry for attention. The act may not be intended for you, personally. It could be that the deliverer of the insult is hurting and needs someone to take time to truly listen to what is being said. They may just be having a bad day. If you insist on matching words, you may be causing more harm than good.

Once they realize you don't intend to respond as they expected, they may think twice the next time.

Change yourself to change your life.

The only person you can truly control is you. Stop focusing on what others can do to change your life. Start with the person you see in the mirror and go from there. Look further inward and assess your own habits and actions. Determine what you can do to make your own life better.

Spend some time researching self-help and motivational books, tapes, courses, and other media. Make a commitment to yourself to be the best human being you can possibly be. Don't wait for someone else to point out your weaknesses or strengths. Discover them yourself and get to work on what needs to change, improve, or be eliminated.

Accepting weakness shows strength.

If you can accept your weaknesses, you can overcome them. The very act of acceptance requires strength — not physical, but mental.

Put your mind to the task of acknowledging that you are not strong in all areas, nor should you be. However, when you know where your strengths and weaknesses are, you can compensate for your weaknesses, thereby showing strength.

"But he said to me, 'My grace is sufficient for you, for my power is made perfect in weakness.' Therefore I will boast all the more gladly about my weaknesses, so that Christ's power may rest on me."

— 2 Corinthians 12:9

Unresolved anger, deep within you, is not hidden. It is revealed in your thoughts, words, and actions. It controls your very existence.

Unresolved anger can be seen in your mannerisms and responses to others. You owe it to yourself and others to determine what is causing your inward anger. It could be a childhood experience or a relationship gone wrong. Perhaps you need to find out more about why you think what you think or do what you do. You might consider getting a personality test and studying the resulting analysis. Or, you may consider pursuing counseling.

Whatever you decide, let it be to do something to harness the anger and use it in a more positive manner.

You ALWAYS have a choice and the choice is yours.

We all have choices. We make them everyday. We choose when to get up in the morning and when to go to bed at night. We choose to do something or nothing. We choose to be the best or average. We choose to give or take or both.

Every choice involves options that we sometimes don't consider and this leads us to believe we don't have a choice. Think about how you get through your day. You have probably convinced yourself that you have to do this or that. In fact, life is full of choices but you need to consider them more fully rather than just doing what comes naturally or what you've always done.

Think about it. The choice is yours.

Simple acts of kindness are like boomerangs – they come back to you.

When you show kindness to others, it's bound to be returned to you in some form or measure. It may not be reciprocated by the same person but you will see it again. Simple acts of kindness may be a smile, a helping hand, a friendly greeting, lending an ear, expressions of sympathy, saying , "Please" and "Thank you", or just being there. You have probably already experienced these things from others and have even extended them yourself. Stop and make the connection. Each act extended returns in the manner in which it is delivered—more or less.

Start casting boomerangs of kindness and watch for them to return to you.

Trust is KEY.

Not only is it important for you to trust yourself and others, it's important for others to trust you. If you are to accomplish anything in life, trust will be involved. The dictionary defines trust using words like confidence, reliance, faith, and dependability. Think of instances when these characteristics apply. In every facet of our lives there is a need for trust. Children should be able to trust adults as well as their peers. Spouses should trust one another—it's key for marital harmony. Employers want to trust employees as they must entrust the work to them. Employees want to trust employers to treat them fairly and without discrimination. Friends trust friends to keep their confidences and they rely on each other to be there when needed. Parents want to trust that their teenagers will do the right thing in difficult situations.

Knowledge and proof of these things build trust. You become trustworthy by doing the things others trust you to do. A single violation of this trust could require complete rebuilding.

Once you understand the importance of being trustworthy and accept it as a way of life, other areas of your character will be strengthened and you will be able to better withstand whatever scrutiny you receive.

Dependability

Confidence

Reliability

Truthfulness

Faithfulness

Trustworthiness

Trust

Key

Of central or basic importance.

A promise kept enhances trust.

Keep your promises. Don't make promises you can't or don't intend to keep. Spouses, children, parents, and friends tend to lose trust when promises are constantly broken. On the other hand, when you do your best to keep your promises, or you don't practice making promises you know you can't or won't keep, you raise the level of trust others place in you.

The next time you want to make a promise, think about what it involves and whether or not you have the means and intent to carry it out.

Honesty matters.

Being honest means being truthful. When you're honest you have credibility. Your efforts are seen to be genuine. When you speak, others listen and believe what you say. Honesty helps to foster trust and makes a difference when interacting with others.

When you are younger, you may not think honesty is as important as you will when you get older. Perhaps you feel/felt that if nobody knows, there is no harm. But, as you get older and have more responsibility, you may come to realize just how much it does matter.

When you are honest with yourself as well as others, you make a statement that you are willing to accept both the benefits and consequences of your behavior. It matters to others when they don't have to question your integrity. It should matter to you.

"...whatever is true, whatever is noble, whatever is right, whatever is pure, whatever is lovely, whatever is admirable— if anything is excellent or praiseworthy— think on these things."
— Philippians 4:8

Reach for your dreams, even if you have to stand on your tip-toes.

If you believe in your dreams, do what it takes to make them come true. Make sacrifices, take risks, reach beyond your current grasp. Don't let anything or anyone discourage you from pursuing your dreams. Believe in yourself and find ways to accomplish goals leading to your dreams.

Find role models whose stories are similar to yours. Do your homework about whatever it is you want to accomplish. Be relentless—always keeping your prize in sight.

If you falter, get back up and keep going. Failure should only serve to teach, not discourage. Many of the greats failed numerous times before succeeding. Think of what we might be missing if they had given up on their dreams. Think of what gains there are when you succeed.

Stand tall and reach high!

PART II

Original Poetry

Poetry in my mind sings the songs of my heart...

Chapter 2

Open your mind

What's in your mind determines who you are and how you behave. If you close your mind to certain possibilities, there are fewer to consider. When your mind is open, you are willing to consider that anything is possible. Tasks become more doable and you are less stressed because you believe things can work out for you.

The following selections of original poetry will give you something to think about as you continue on your journey to become a more open-minded individual.

Consider the possibilities

The Lesson

Fate steered us right,
Though pain to each is caused.
We must fight through it,
Until we arrive THERE.

THERE is where we belong.
A state, a place, with or without
The things we desire or the fears we face.

We BELONG together,
Though painful it may be.
A lesson is being taught
That we must learn -
Before we can arrive.

Open up and let the learning take place.
The journey slows to closed
minds and hearts.

Come to me, take me to you.
Hold me close, touch me gently,
Speak kindly, look softly, and you'll see...

The Lesson is LOVE!

Stop the Anger!

Angry woman,
Cool your heels.
Count to ten.
See how it feels.

Angry man,
Love your wife.
Give her a hug.
Change your life.

Angry children,
Stop the fuss.
Obey your parents.
Do what you must.

<u>Fate</u>

I see your hurt;
I feel your pain;
It's like the storm
With all the rain.

Dry your eyes and lift your head;
Stand up tall and don't you dread.
There are brighter days if you just wait.
Go to your destiny – meet your fate.

For Everything A Reason

Her heart aches for want of arms to hold her
Simply because she needs a hug...

She longs to hear kind words to let her know that
she does not cause the anger...

She walks on eggshells just so she does not disturb
others
While they are preoccupied...

Her house is full, yet she feels all alone.
Their wants have over-shadowed their needs.

They are ruled by these desires, yet
Enslaved by their fears of each other.

How long will it last?
When will her family start to be?
Was it really meant to be?

God does not make mistakes!
Keep searching for the reason for as long as it takes.

It's ALWAYS there.

There is a time for everything, and a season for every activity under heaven..."

— Ecclesiastes 3:1

<u>A Need to Know?</u>

I wish that I could plainly see
All the things in store for me.

My hopes and dreams and all those things --
The opportunities that living brings.

My family, friends, and all they need;
The things that make us follow and lead.

Should I pass on before it's done,
I'll not regret a single one
Of all the things that helped me know
The way that I was meant to go.

Optimism/Pessimism

Optimism is its own reward.
It's much like when we draw a lucky card.
It helps us realize our hopes and dreams,
And the task-at-hand is easier than it seems.

Pessimism seeks to bring us down,
And makes our face a constant, gloomy frown.
It strips us of our hopes and dreams,
And takes away our drive and self-esteem.

Just realize the choice is yours to make.
Be careful that it's not a big mistake.
For one will make your life a living hell.
The other will keep you happy and living well.

Which do you choose?

Boundaries

Boundaries are necessary
To keep our kids from harm.
We set them up like sand-to-sea
So they feel safe and warm.

They may roar and may rebel
But we must stand steadfast.
The lessons we teach today
Are truly the ones that last.

Boundaries are also set
To keep us in our place,
And help us know the way to go
In returning to our base.

We sometimes try to reach beyond
The line He drew for us;
And He is there to let us know
That all we need is trust.

Sometimes He may allow us
To stretch beyond that line;
This only serves to help us see
His truth is most divine.

For when the right time comes along
To move beyond His mark
We will know the journey upon which
He leads us to embark.

Undisputed

He lives inside his head all day
And rarely sleeps at night;
Keeps to himself and speaks few words
For survival he will fight.

Inside his world, he is the champ –
An undisputed fact.
Each challenger will realize
It's more that just an act.

Outside his world, he's not well-known;
For who out there would care
About a man condemned to hell
Where violence is not rare?

A man who lives inside his head
Never fears the day
When someone else can take him down
And take his crown away.

Until that day, he stays within
With a discipline you can't refute.
He's the champ and this, for sure,
Is a fact you can't dispute.

<u>Angels</u>

I believe in Angels.
I can feel them all around.
They're up above, in the air,
And also on the ground.

Angels help us deal with life.
They help us see the light
Throughout the dark when we can't see
They get us through the night.

If someone comes to lend a hand
Whenever you're in need,
You can know, be sure of this,
It was an Angel, indeed.

Angels come in many forms
It might just be your pet.
Or they may look like you or me,
Your doctor or the vet.

Be careful how you look at life
And all those that you meet.
Don't be so quick to challenge things –
There is an Angel at your feet.

Angel
A typically benevolent celestial being that acts as an intermediary between heaven and earth.

— American Heritage Dictionary

"*See that you do not look down on one of these little ones. For I tell you that their angels in heaven always see the face of my Father in heaven*"

— Matthew 18:10

<u>Lessons Learned?</u>

When we are young we think we know it all.
No one can tell us we're not ten feet tall.
We think the world owes us so much more
Than we are willing to work or even pay for.

As we get older, we remain a bit misguided;
Believing we can get through life undecided
About the things we must do in order to succeed.
We still refuse to listen and take heed.

Still older yet, we try to act so wise.
Hoping others won't see it in our eyes –
The fact that we did not each opportunity seize
When we were younger and doing as we please.

You look around for someone else to blame –
To those who have achieved fortune and fame.
You try to say "No one gave me a chance."
But it was you who simply refused to dance.

Life is full of lessons each and every day.
It's up to you to learn along the way.
An open mind is Oh so very key
If you are to fulfill your destiny.

Chapter 3

Open your heart

Once you have opened your mind to other possibilities, you are ready to open your heart to feelings. This is almost a natural progression. When you have a positive outlook and an open mind, your heart will be open to emotions you never knew you had.

The collection that follows will help you to feel things differently than perhaps you usually do.

Feel the possibilities

Kindness

Kindness costs you nothing,
Yet, it can buy more than silver, gold, or even money.

Kindness can only be given, never taken –
Once received, it becomes a torch to be passed on.

Kindness is a blanket that warms the heart.

Kindness can heal the hurt
Or ease the pain;
Soothe the soul
Or cool the flames;
Bring a smile
Or dry a tear;
Brighten a mood
Or calm a fear.

Kindness can come from stranger or friend,
Small acts or big ones, all to the same end.

You can give and receive kindness and so can I.
If more of us give it more will receive it.

Don't wait another minute,
It's simple to do
You to me, me to you.
Try a smile or lend a hand.
Give a ride or share what you can.
Kiss your kids or hug your love.
Give a wink or mend a glove.

Kindness makes a difference...

"An anxious heart weighs a man down, but a kind word cheers him up."
                                    Proverbs 3:25

"Pleasant words are a honeycomb, sweet to the soul and healing to the bones."
                                    Proverbs 16:24

With Each New Day

As I am blessed with each new day,
I have a talk with God.
And thank Him for the gift of life
that He chose to impart.

I thank Him for His company
throughout my busy day.
I thank Him for the discipline
that He has sent my way.

I thank Him for my health, strength,
courage, and well-being.
I thank Him for necessities
such as walking, talking, seeing.

I thank Him for the mind not wasted
on idle, useless things.
I thank Him for my patience and
the good things that it brings.

I thank Him for the kind exchange
between me and the stranger.
I thank Him for the many times
that I was slow to anger.

And when my day begins again,
I say another prayer.
I thank God for the loving ways
that He shows me He cares.

If

If I could say to you
What my heart has said to me,
I could put your mind at ease
And then our lives would be
Truly intertwined
As one
As we become
The soul of our very BEING.

If I could only make you see
That my life is you and me
Outside, inside, in between,
You, me, and everything.
Our hopes and dreams
The times we share,
The love we give,
The ways we care.
Opening our eyes and SEEING.

If I could give to you the things
That I think you deserve
I would soon exhaust my supply
And there would be no reserve.

For I think you should have
The World,
The sun, the moon, the stars,
Your girl,

Your one and only,
Your terribly lonely
Your life,
Your world,
Your family,
Your Sweet,
Marie

The many roles we play...

Is That Really Me?

Who was I?
Where did I go?
I've searched and searched
Still I don't know.

Where was I?
What did I do?
Did you know me?
Did I know you?

Daughter, sister, cousin, friend,
Mother, wife, all I've been.
All these roles I've had to play,
Year in, year out, day-by-day.

The time has passed before I knew it,
The ones I am and have been to do it,
All within a short life span,
While being held in the palm of His hand.

<u>Without Words?</u>

I cannot envision myself without our hope
Or expectation of communication.
For as long as we have been acquainted
This particular part of me absconds vacation.

To say you've grown to be
so very much a part of me
Is to understate the beauty and importance
of our greatest tree.

No, what you've come to mean to me
is so very hard to explain
Without the aid of words and phrases
which appear to me only in vain.

So many fine phrases are battling
even now within my mind
To come forward and serve the purpose of not merely
indicating to you the very importance of this time.

Elaborating on this to you
Would not really be a most pressing thing to do.

See, what I'm trying to say
is that our lives really changed when we met that fortunate day.

To simply say I love you
would nearly be enough;
To say I really need you is
less that poetic "buff".

But then, to say I love you, need you, want you
with consideration attached—
And add affection – strive for your eternal presence -
Well words and emotion are very nearly evenly
matched.

Who can verbally express emotion so strong and deep
-seated as yours and mine?
It can only truly manifest itself with the help of the
endless and constant revolution of the wheels of time.

The Circle of Love

The circle of love is unbroken
Because we each proceed
To reach out to another
Whenever we see a need.

Should one decide to falter
The next cannot move on.
He has no hand to hold him
Or push him further along.

Reach out to help another
Every day you live;
And someone else will help you
When it comes his time to give.

Don't let the circle be broken.
We all can use the love.
And remember that it all started
With the Glorious One above.

What You Mean To Me

A loving glance that tells me you still care;
Remembering the happy times we share;

A simple touch that says "I'm glad you're here."
A reassuring voice that allays my fear;

A confidence that says "I know you can."
A willingness to always lend a hand;

A tender kiss upon my lips each day;
As I must leave and go my separate way;

A smiling face to greet each workday's end;
A comforting and everlasting friend;

As time goes by revealing the mystery
Of life and love and all that's meant to be—
These things – and more – you'll always mean to me.

Everyone Has a Story to Tell

Everyone has a story to tell.
It's what we're all about.
Our life and times kept safe inside.
Do we want to let it out?

Ordinary or extraordinary,
We can weigh them all the same.
For we are all born and we all die
You don't have to know their name.

When you see a stranger on the street,
Don't pass without a thought
Of how they've lived and who they are
Or what their life's about.

Pain and suffering or joy of life—
It's all right there to see.
If we look past the outer core
We'll think, "They're just like me."

<u>Within My Heart</u>

Take my hand, come go with me,
and live within my heart.
As long as you remain there,
I know we'll never part.

The love we have was meant to be
for as long as there is air
For us to breathe as we begin
a life we promised to share.

The ups and downs, the good and bad
will only serve to be
A source of strength and fortitude
for our new formed family.

I'll take your hand, my precious one,
to you my heart I'll give;
Remain there within, my love,
for as long as we both shall live.

We're All They Have Left

As children close their eyes at night
and say their little prayer,
They know that when the morning comes,
their family will still be there.

If, when the sun comes up again,
and all is as they asked,
They breathe a sigh of sweet relief
that things are still in tact.

But, if they wake and no one's there
whose face they recognize,
They turn their heads, squeeze real tight,
then reopen their eyes.

Their hearts will sink and despair will grip their mind,
body, and soul,
As they realize they've been left alone
with no loved ones to hold.

Now we the rest must care enough
for those suffering this ill.
We're all they have and God above
has given us His will.

So take a hand and lead them on
– they have a lifetime to try
And make the best of this tragedy
they'll relive as time goes by.

For all our lives have now been touched
by such a senseless act;
But hand-in-hand, united we stand,
we'll make the journey back.

Written in memory of the children left behind as a result of September 11, 2001

―――――――――――――――――――――――――

"... the God of all comfort, who comforts us in all our troubles, so that we can comfort those in any trouble with the comfort we ourselves have received from God. For just as the sufferings of Christ flow into our lives, so also through Christ our comfort overflows."

— 2 Corinthians 1:3-5

Chapter 4

Open Your Mind
And
Open Your Heart

As you continue this journey of self-discovery and self-improvement, you will arrive at a place where you have successfully opened both your heart and mind. You will be prepared to accept all of life's stages — including death. You will come to realize that it is inevitable and preparation and acceptance are key in leaving a legacy for your loved ones.

The final pieces included on the following pages are for you to consider in completing your journey.

Experience the possibilities

My Time Is Done

My time on Earth was what it was meant to be;
No more or less than anyone's, you see.

When we are born, our time is already set;
No matter what we do or say, that is all we get.

For some it may be minutes;
For others a few days or even years.
Whatever we are given,
We must welcome it with cheers.

No matter how many or few,
Life still goes too fast;
So whatever you choose to do with yours,
Try to leave something that will last.

For me, I leave you memories of how I tried to live,
With love and care for you and others and all I tried
to give.

So grieve for me if you must,
But not too long, dear one.
For if you believe and trust in God,
You'll know my time here is done.

My Reward

Today, I see my death as a wonderful reward,
As my Lord brings me closest to His heart.

I'm finally going home to take my rest,
Knowing now that I have done my best.

I realized my purpose in life early on,
The reason to this world that I was born.

I was chosen by the Lord above,
To touch the lives of those I know and love,
In a way that would stay with them forever,
And help them all to reach a higher level.

My work was fulfilling and sometimes took its toll,
While I pressed on to reach this final goal.

And now that I have given it my all,
I know at last that I have heard the call,
Telling me it's time to pass the torch,
And stand relieved of this, my final watch.

I know you all will grieve and cry for me.
But just remember how I came to be --
Living in this place for this brief time --
And keep this memory in your heart and mind.

— For Jackie

Epilogue...

<u>Life Through Books</u>

She's always buying books to read
She has a desperate need
To learn all she can of life
And cure the world of strife.

Most of the time she feels content
As books are such good friends.
But reality strikes and brings her back
To a life of constant amends.

Energy's up and then it's down
How does she cope with it
And all the things she tries to do
To keep herself well-fit.

Her life is split between so much
She tries so hard to please
Her family, friends, and everyone
Until she's ill-at-ease.

Heart and mind just open up
To let hurt and happiness in
Sometimes it's good, sometimes it's bad
But with it she does contend.

So off she goes to get a book
To answer what she asks
It's what she knows will do the trick
And put her back on task.

After Word

I truly hope you have enjoyed this book as much as I enjoyed sharing it. It is my sincere desire that, after reading these words, you will think more seriously about being more positive and enjoying a life of fulfillment from this journey.

Don't let the journey stop here. This is only a beginning. Continue to search for ways to learn more about yourself — who you are; why you behave the way you do; what makes you happy; what your true purpose is in life.

NOTES

Additional Resources

The following books and tapes have contributed to my journey and may prove useful to you in your journey of self-discovery.

Stephen R. Covey
- The Seven Habits of Highly Effective People
- First Things First (with A. Roger Merrill and Rebecca R. Merrill)
- Living the 7 Habits
- Principle-Centered Leadership

Don Miguel Ruiz
- The Four Agreements
- The Four Agreements Companion Book
- The Mastery of Love

Dr. Phil McGraw
- Life Strategies
- Getting Real
- Self Matters

Gary Zukav
- The Seat of the Soul
- Soul Stories

Dr. Viktor E. Frankl
- Man's Search for Meaning

Dr. Tom Bay
- Change Your Attitude
- Look Within or Do Without

Sarah Ban Breathnach
- Simple Abundance
- Simple Abundance Companion
- Something More
- A Man's Journey to Simple Abundance

Carol Adrienne
- The Purpose of Your Life

Les Brown
- Live Your Dreams

T.D. Jakes
- Maximize the Moment

Denis Waitley
- The Psychology of Winning

Brian Tracy
- The Psychology of Achievement

Gary R. Collins
- You Can Make a Difference

Dr. Mark Thurston and Christopher Fazel
- The Edgar Cayce Handbook for Creating Your Future

Jay McGraw
- Life Strategies for Teens
- Closing the Gap

Sean Covey
- Seven Habits of Highly Effective Teens

Cheryl Richardson
- Take Time for Your Life
- Life Makeovers

Florence Littauer
- It Takes So Little to Be Above Average
- Your Personality Tree

Dr. John M. Oldham and Lois B. Morris
- The New Personality Self-Portrait—Why You Think, Work, Love, and Act the Way You Do

Bob Greene and Oprah Winfrey
- Make the Connection

James Redfield
- The Celestine Prophecy
- The Tenth Insight
- The Celestine Prophecy: An Experiential Guide

ORDER FORM

W. Marie Giles
P.O. Box 3757
Pensacola, FL 32516-3757

Open Your Mind, Open Your Heart
A collection of words of wisdom, heartfelt thoughts, and original poetry

Please send me ___ copies of **Open Your Mind, Open Your Heart** at $16.95 per copy. Add $3.00 for shipping and handling. Make check or money order payable to Willie M. Giles. Allow 4 weeks for delivery.

☐ Check/Money Order Enclosed

Please send the book(s) I have requested to:

_____
Name (Please print)

_____
Address

_____
City   State   Zip

_____
Phone (include area code)

www.ingramcontent.com/pod-product-compliance
Lightning Source LLC
Chambersburg PA
CBHW070053120426
42742CB00048B/2513